Who Works Here?

Fire Station

by Lola M. Schaefer

Heinemann Library
Chicago, Illinois

© 2001 Reed Educational & Professional Publishing
Published by Heinemann Library,
an imprint of Reed Educational & Professional Publishing,
100 N. LaSalle, Suite 1010
Chicago, IL 60602
Customer Service 888-454-2279
Visit our website at www.heinemannlibrary.com

Designed by Wilkinson Design
Printed in Hong Kong

05 04 03 02 01
10 9 8 7 6 5 4 3 2 1

Library of Congress Cataloging-in-Publication Data
Schaefer, Lola M., 1950-
    Fire station / by Lola M. Schaefer.
      p. cm. -- (Who works here?)
    Includes bibliographical references and index.
    ISBN 1-58810-126-6 (lb)
    1. Fire departments--Officials and employees--Juvenile literature. 2. Fire
fighters--Juvenile literature. 3. Fire prevention--Juvenile literature. [1. Fire departments.
2. Fire fighters. 3. Occupations.] I. Title.

TH9158 .S33 2001
363.37 -dc21

363,37

00-058085

Acknowledgments
Photography by Phil Martin and Kimberly Saar.
Special thanks to Captain Brian Duff and all the workers at the fire department in Fort Wayne, Indiana, and to workers everywhere who take pride in what they do.

Some words are shown in bold, **like this.**
You can find out what they mean by looking in the glossary.

Contents

What Is a Fire Station?

Fire stations help keep communities safe around the United States.

A fire station is a building where firefighters live and work when on duty. While at the fire station, firefighters clean and test the fire trucks and equipment. They file reports on past emergencies and train to stay prepared. They cook, eat, and sleep at the fire station, too.

Firefighters are trained to **respond** quickly to fires, rescues, and **medical** emergencies. They know that time can save a **citizen's** life or home.

This fire station is in Fort Wayne, Indiana. This map shows where the people in this book work. Many fire stations in the United States look like this.

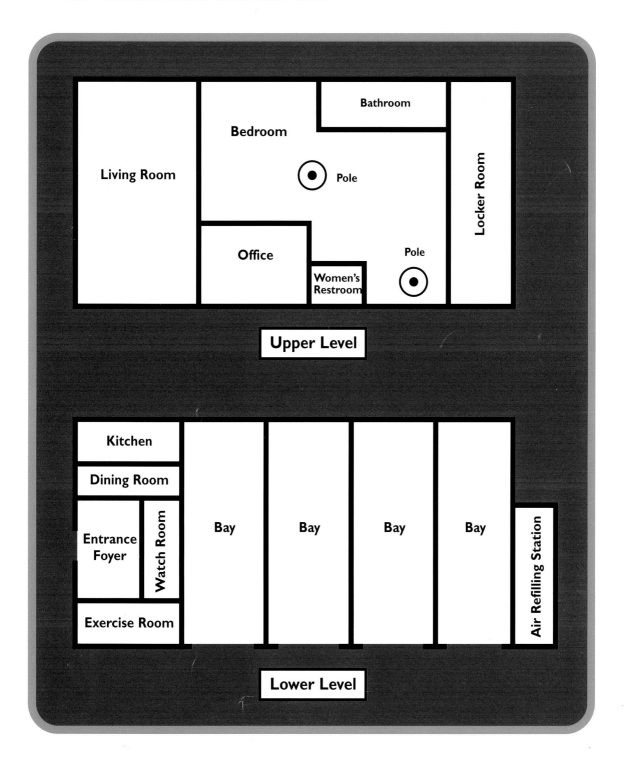

Firefighter

To become a firefighter, a person first attends firefighter training for six months. Then, the student attends the Fire Academy. Here, each person goes through **medical** training and special firefighting training, including the use of fire trucks and equipment.

Carlos, a firefighter, tests the jaws-of-life. This piece of equipment frees people trapped in car accidents.

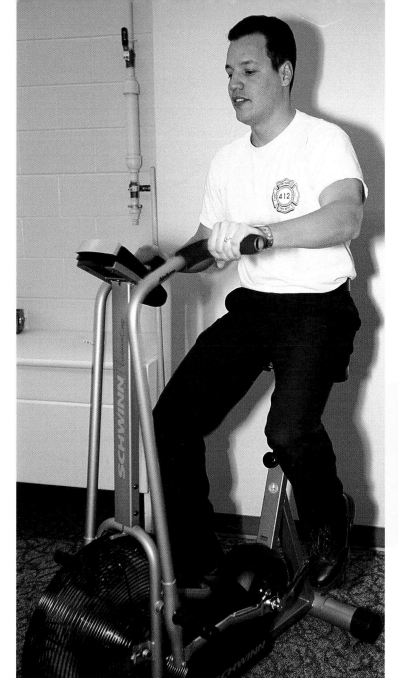

While on duty, firefighters can keep fit by working out in the gym in the fire station.

When the fire alarm sounds, firefighters dress in their bunker gear within 30 seconds. In the truck, they add their air tanks and receive their duties for the emergency **scene.** They safely arrive at the scene within three minutes.

Captain

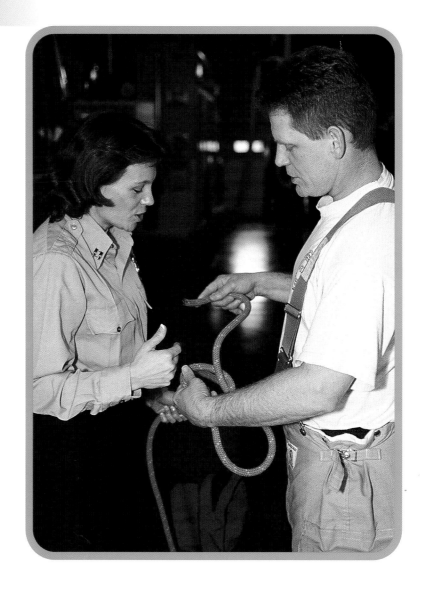

Mimi, the fire station captain, trains a new firefighter on the use of ropes and knots.

A fire station captain works with a crew of firefighters. During their work shift, the captain makes sure the crew knows how to use all the fire and **medical** equipment. The captain leads the firefighters in special training for emergency calls.

The captain rides next to the driver in the fire truck and takes information about the fire from the radio.

Most captains of fire stations have been firefighters for 5-10 years. They receive special training to become a captain. The captain of a fire station and crew care about one another. They work together like a family.

Fire Chief

The fire chief is responsible for everything that happens in the fire department. Each month, the chief attends different meetings with crew members from the fire department, police department, and city. Together they plan ways to keep **citizens** safe.

Tim is the fire chief. He and his crew are talking about firefighting safety.

Usually the mayor of the city chooses the fire chief. A firefighter works about 10-15 years in the fire department before becoming chief. Tim, like many fire chiefs, is a strong leader who helps his crew do their best work.

Here, Fire Chief Tim makes notes on his computer for his next officer meeting.

Using Fire Trucks

After a fire, firefighters store their equipment on the truck, ready for the next emergency call.

When **responding** to a house fire, firefighters drive pump trucks, ladder trucks, and rescue trucks. An ambulance, two district chiefs, and the arson investigators meet them at the **scene.** Everyone has their duties and they begin work immediately. Teamwork helps put out a fire quickly.

A firefighter can use a fire truck to pump water from a fire hydrant or the tank on the truck. Fire trucks carry hundreds of gallons of water. The **nozzle** on the end of the hose can spray 1,000 gallons (3,785 liters) a minute. The fire truck driver stays in the truck and keeps the water pumping through the hoses.

At the fire, the fire truck driver uses these controls to pump water through the hoses.

Using Firefighter Gear

Bunker gear is the clothing that protects a firefighter. The helmet, **goggles,** and hood keep heat, steam, smoke, and small objects away from the firefighter's head. The fire-resistant coat and pants prevent heat and water from reaching the firefighter. Gloves and boots protect the firefighter's hands and feet from cuts, heat, and water.

Cory, a firefighter, wears his bunker gear when he answers an emergency call.

Each firefighter carries a hand tool into the **scene** of a fire. An ax cuts doors or walls. A pry bar helps lift heavy objects or pull doors open. Pipe poles pull out screens, break windows, or tear ceilings.

This firefighter is using a pipe pole to pull screens out of a burning building.

Firefighting Safety Equipment

Firefighters wear a Person Alert Safety System, called P.A.S.S. for short. If a firefighter stops moving for 30 seconds, a **motion detector** in the device sets off a loud screeching noise. This noise alerts other firefighters and lets them find the firefighter in need of help.

The P.A.S.S. device clips to the front of firefighter Carlos's coat.

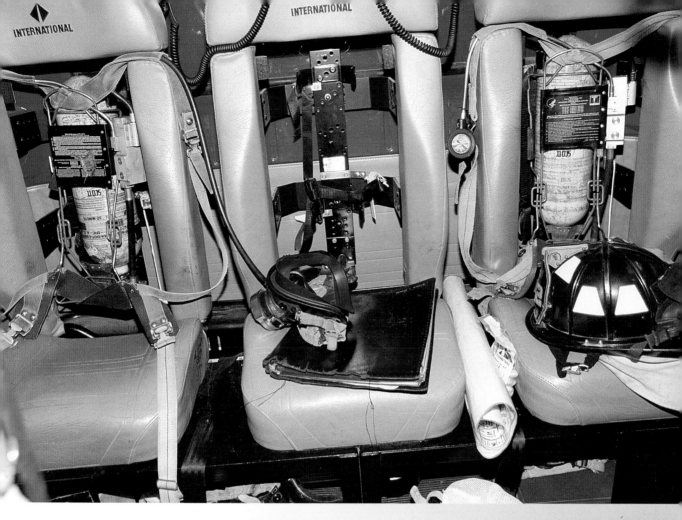

Firefighters keep air-packs and harnesses in the seats
of the fire truck so they can get ready quickly.

Firefighters wear an air-pack at a fire. Each pack has 30
minutes of fresh air. When the air-pack has only five minutes
of fresh air left, the mask **vibrates.** The firefighter then leaves
the fire safely. Outside, the firefighter can change the air
bottle and return to the fire.

Special Operations Teams

The Special Operations Response Team, S.O.R.T. for short, is a group of firefighters trained to help in life rescues. This team has its own trucks and equipment at the fire station. They rescue people caught in low, high, or tight places.

Ron, the district chief of S.O.R.T., checks the straps on a life basket used to rescue injured people.

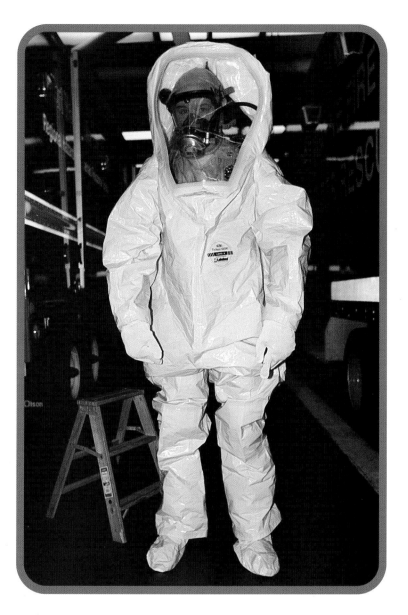

Captain Scott breathes fresh air from an air tank on his back through a mask on his face.

The Haz-Mat Team responds to **hazardous** material emergencies. Each member of the team is a firefighter trained for these emergencies. They have to wear a sealed Haz-Mat suit before entering the **scene.** These suits protect the firefighters from harmful **chemicals** that may hurt their bodies.

Using Special Equipment

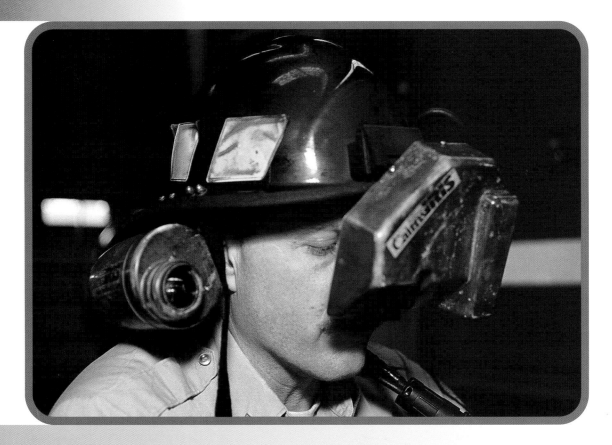

This firefighter looks through the viewing screen to see the room using the Cairns Iris.

The Cairns Iris (karns eye-riss) is a helmet with an **infrared** camera on the side. It helps firefighters see in smoke-filled rooms. The infrared camera shows warm objects, such as people or fire, as bright light. The Cairns Iris helps firefighters find trapped people and hidden fire.

Water rescue equipment helps firefighters with searches and rescues underwater. Extra training teaches firefighters how to use this equipment safely. Firefighters wear a dry suit, a full-face mask, and a tank of fresh air. They may enter rivers, lakes, or ponds looking for people or objects from crimes.

The vest on the dry suit holds cutting tools that a firefighter can use to free people or objects.

Chief of Fire Arson Investigation

The chief of fire arson investigation studies every fire **scene.** He or she decides whether the fire was an accident or arson. When a person sets a fire on purpose, it is called arson. The chief of fire arson investigation can arrest people who commit arson because it is a crime.

Karen is the chief of fire arson investigation. She is talking with a **witness** to a fire to get more information for her report.

The chief of fire arson investigation works with a team of **investigators.** They decide where and how the fire started. Firefighters usually train 750–1,000 hours to become a fire arson investigator. To become a chief, a person usually works at least five years as an investigator.

Arson investigators use science skills to examine the fire scene.

Fire Inspector

A fire inspector visits businesses and schools in the **community.** He or she checks that the buildings meet all **fire codes.** If there are fire **hazards,** the inspector gives the owner 30 days to correct the problems. Then, the fire inspector returns and checks the building again.

Marsha, the fire inspector, records information from her **inspections** on the computer.

Marsha is checking that the sprinkler system in this building is working well.

Fire inspectors are firefighters that attend 50–70 hours of extra training to learn the fire codes. Each inspector must pass a state test to become **certified.** They also attend classes to learn how to check that fire alarms and fire extinguishers work. Fire inspectors want the buildings in a community to be safe.

Public Information Officer

Brian, a public information officer, is telling a reporter about new **fire codes.**

A public information officer tells the news **media** what is happening in the fire department. This person writes news stories, speaks with reporters, and often gives live **interviews.** A public information officer **communicates** with many people every day.

Brian, like other public information officers, visits every fire and emergency **scene.** He speaks with the fire department's district chief and arson investigators. Afterward, he files a report for the local news media listing facts and damages.

At this fire scene, Brian talks with an arson investigator about the cause of the fire.

Dispatcher

If a **citizen** needs the fire department, he or she dials the emergency telephone number. The dispatcher in the dispatch center answers the call and asks for the person's name and the address of the fire or emergency. Then, the dispatcher radios the fire department with this information.

Mike is a dispatcher. He is sending firefighters to the **scene** of a car accident.

Here, Mike shows the location of a house fire to another dispatcher.

Fire department dispatchers receive months of training for their jobs. They learn how to keep the callers calm as they question them. They also learn the **radio codes.** To become a dispatcher, a person needs to pass a test. Dispatchers must show that they can use the communications equipment quickly to help citizens in need.

Glossary

certified able to do a job after passing a test

crew team of people who work together to do a specific job

chemical substance used in chemistry; all things are made of different chemicals

citizen person who lives in a town, city, or country

communicate to trade information, such as by talking or writing

community area where people live, work, and shop

fire codes set of rules for homes, businesses, and schools to help prevent fires

goggles large eyeglasses that fit tightly around the eyes to protect them

hazard danger or risk

hazardous dangerous or risky

infrared light rays that cannot be seen without special equipment; they give off heat that can be felt

inspection official check of something

interview meeting at which someone is asked questions

investigator person trained to find out as much as possible about something

mayor leader of a town or city

media different things that give information; newspapers, magazines, radio, and TV

medical to do with health or medicine

motion detector device that is programmed to do something because of movement

nozzle spout that directs the flow of liquid from the end of a hose

radio codes words, letters, symbols, or numbers used instead of ordinary words to send messages on an emergency radio

respond react to a call, warning, or announcement

scene place where something happens

screen surface showing pictures or information, like on a TV

vibrate move back and forth quickly

witness person who has seen or heard something

More Books to Read

Bowman-Kruhm, Mary. *A Day in the Life of a Firefighter.* New York, N.Y.: The Rosen Publishing Group, Inc., 1997.

Greene, Carol. *Firefighters Fight Fires.* Chanhassen, Minn.: The Child's World, Inc., 1996.

Kallen, Stuart A. *The Fire Station.* Edina, Minn.: ABDO Publishing Company, 1997.

Schomp, Virginia. *If You Were a Firefighter.* Tarrytown, N.Y.: Marshall Cavendish Corporation, 2000.

Index